Earthquakes

Keith Lye

RSVP

RAINTREE
STECK-VAUGHN
P U B L I S H E R S
The Steck-Vaughn Company

Austin, Texas

Series Editor: A. Patricia Sechi
Editor: Ambreen Husain and
  Claire Llewellyn
Project Manager: Joyce Spicer
Electronic Production:
  Scott Melcer
Artwork: Alex Pang
Cover artwork: Alex Pang
Picture Research:
  Ambreen Husain
Educational Advisor:
  Joy Richardson

Library of Congress Cataloging-in-Publication Data
Lye, Keith.
    Earthquakes / Keith Lye.
      p.   cm. — (First starts)
    Includes index.
    Summary: Discusses the phenomenon of earthquakes, how and where they can occur, what causes them, the damage they can create, and how they can be predicted.
    ISBN 0-8114-3409-5
    1. Earthquakes — Juvenile literature. [1. Earthquakes.]
I. Title.   II. Series.
QE521.3.L94   1993
551.2'2—dc20   92-31816
                              CIP AC
Printed and bound in the United States by Lake Book, Melrose Park, IL

1 2 3 4 5 6 7 8 9 0 LB 98 97 96 95 94 93

Contents

What Are Earthquakes?

In some parts of the world without any warning, the ground may suddenly begin to shake or crack open. The shaking may last for a minute or more and can cause a lot of damage. Buildings may fall and people may be killed. This is an **earthquake**. It happens when rocks under the land or the ocean begin to move.

▽ Earthquakes are frightening. They can cause a lot of damage.

What Causes Earthquakes?

The **Earth** seems solid and still, but it is not. Below its surface it is so hot that some rocks melt. The hard **crust** on the outside of the Earth is the ground we live on. It is cracked in places. The cracks are called faults. Rocks may suddenly slip along a fault and cause an earthquake.

▷ Cracks in the Earth's crust are called faults.

▽ Blocks of rock sometimes move up and down along a fault.

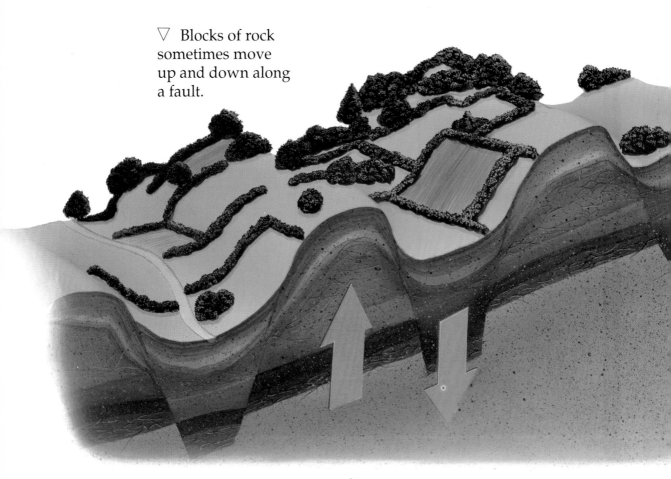

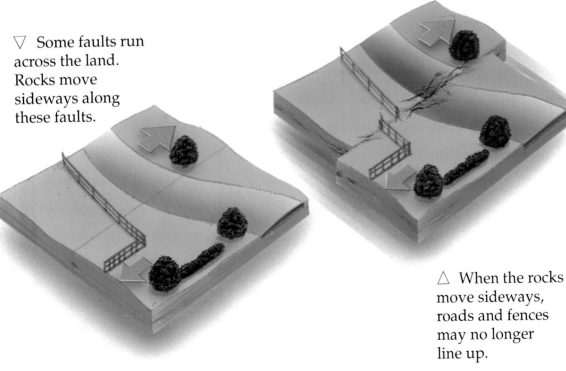

▽ Some faults run across the land. Rocks move sideways along these faults.

△ When the rocks move sideways, roads and fences may no longer line up.

How Strong Are Earthquakes?

There are about 500,000 earthquakes every year. Most of them are so small that people do not notice them. Many are under the ocean far from land.

About one earthquake in every five is felt by people. A thousand earthquakes cause damage each year. A few very strong ones do a great deal of harm.

▽ Small earthquakes may make drinks shake in cups and glasses.

▷ Big earthquakes make the ground move like a ship's deck in stormy weather.

▷ The strongest earthquakes damage buildings. People may be killed.

Earthquake Zones

The strongest earthquakes are found in earthquake zones. These are the places where huge pieces of the Earth's cracked crust are moving. The pieces of crust are called **plates**. They fit together like a jigsaw puzzle, but are shifted around by the movements of hot liquid rock inside the Earth.

▽ The city of San Francisco, California, is in an earthquake zone.

◁ The Earth's crust is cracked into big pieces called plates.

▽ The Earth's main earthquake zones lie around the edges of the plates.

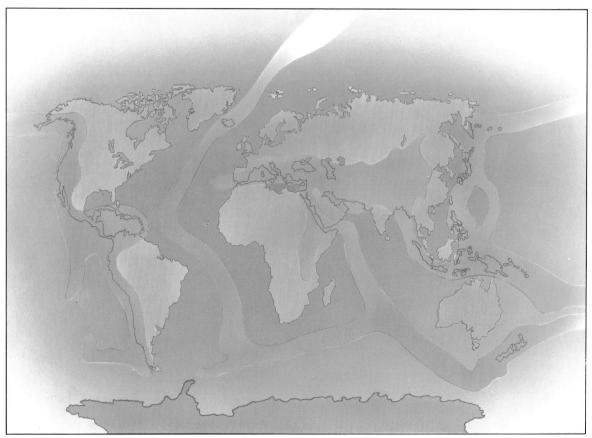

Earthquakes Under the Ocean

Many mountains rise from the seafloor. They may form long mountain ranges that are hidden beneath the waves. In the middle of the ranges are deep **valleys**. These are the edges of the Earth's plates. The plates are moving slowly apart. When they move, the seafloor shakes. Hot, runny rock rises from inside the earth to fill any cracks.

▷ Hot rock rose from the seafloor and formed a new island called Surtsey.

▽ Mountain ranges rise from the seafloor. In the middle of these are the edges of the Earth's plates.

▷ As the plates move apart, hot, runny rock rises up to fill the cracks.

▽ Plates move apart. The ground shakes, causing an earthquake.

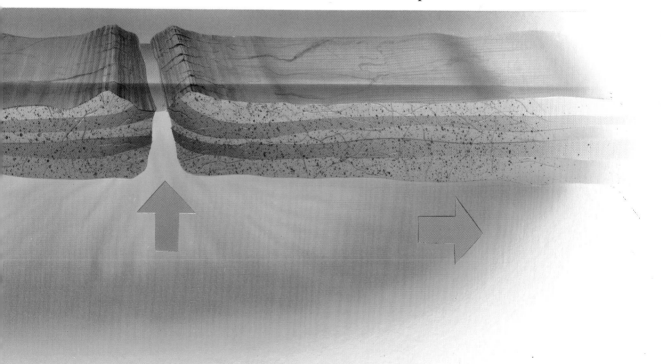

Colliding Plates

Earthquakes under the ocean are caused in different ways. Some of the Earth's plates meet in the deepest parts of the ocean. They push against each other, until one plate is pushed down under the other. Plates do not move smoothly. They collide and jam together. In time, the rocks break and the plates move. These sudden movements cause strong earthquakes.

▷ Tokyo, in Japan, is near one of the deepest parts of the Pacific Ocean. Several plates meet here and cause earthquakes.

▽ When plates push against each other, one will move under the other. This causes an earthquake.

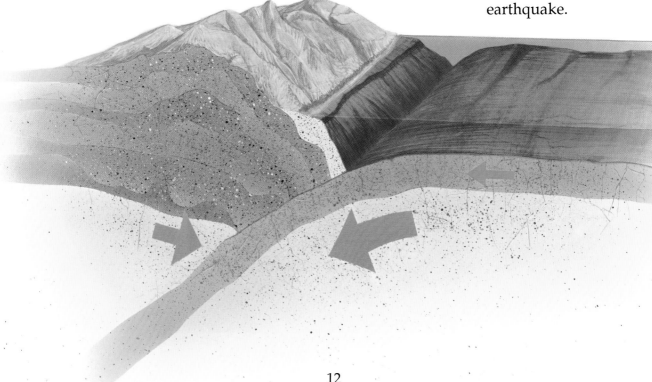

Earthquakes on Land

The edges of most of the moving plates are hidden under the ocean, but some of them are on land.

The edge of two plates runs through California. It is a long crack in the ground called the San Andreas Fault. Movements of the plates along this fault cause earthquakes felt in the cities of Los Angeles and San Francisco.

▷ The San Andreas Fault is in California, where two plates are moving alongside each other.

▷ A sudden movement on the San Andreas Fault in 1906 caused a great earthquake in San Francisco.

Earthquake Damage

Earthquakes may shake buildings and bridges until they fall down. People are sometimes buried under the **rubble**. Another danger is fire because gas pipes may break or stoves may fall over. Fire fighters and other rescue services help people after an earthquake.

▽ Bridges may collapse in an earthquake. Vehicles may be crushed.

◁ Rescuers try to save people trapped in the rubble after an earthquake.

▽ Earthquakes often start fires. Fire fighters work to put out the flames.

Avalanches and Landslides

When there are earthquakes in the mountains, the ground shakes, and loose snow and ice start to slide down the steep slopes. This is called an **avalanche**. Avalanches may knock over trees and bury houses and people. Sometimes, loose rocks, soil, and mud start to roll downhill. This is called a landslide.

▷ An avalanche buried Yungay in 1970. It destroyed fields and houses.

▽ Yungay was a mountain village in South America.

Dangerous Waves

When earthquakes occur under the ocean, they disturb the ocean water. Huge fast-moving waves batter the **coasts**. They may sweep ships inland and drown people on the shore. These waves are called tsunamis. "Tsunami" is the name Japanese people gave these strong waves that sometimes batter their country.

▷ Tsunamis strike the land with great force. They sweep boats far inland.

▽ Tsunamis are huge waves that are caused by earthquakes. They can do a lot of damage.

Studying Earthquakes

The study of earthquakes is called **seismology**, and people who study them are called **seismologists**. They use instruments called **seismographs** to record even the smallest earthquakes. Seismographs contain a weight hanging from a frame. If the ground shakes, the frame moves, but the weight stays still. The movement of the frame is recorded.

▽ This is an old Chinese instrument. When the land moves during an earthquake, balls fall into a toad's mouth.

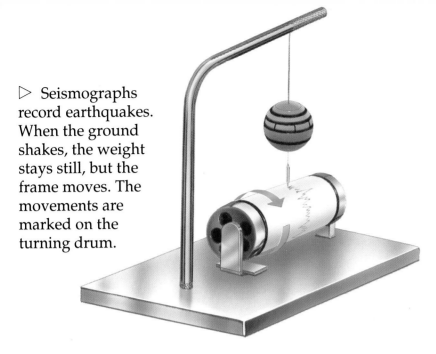

▷ Seismographs record earthquakes. When the ground shakes, the weight stays still, but the frame moves. The movements are marked on the turning drum.

▽ Scientists study earthquakes all around the world.

Animals and Earthquakes

In China scientists have noticed that animals often behave strangely before an earthquake. Chickens and horses run around frightened, pandas moan, and snakes come out of the ground. Perhaps the animals can feel things happening inside the Earth that we cannot feel.

△ Chickens flap their wings and cluck loudly before an earthquake.

◁ Horses sometimes whinny and rear up just before an earthquake.

▷ Dogs seem to sense that something is wrong.

Forecasting an Earthquake

Scientists are saving people's lives by **forecasting** earthquakes. In 1975 scientists in China predicted an earthquake in the city of Haicheng. They asked people to leave the city shortly before it was hit. But scientists have failed to forecast other earthquakes. Now they study all the changes that take place in the ground before an earthquake.

▷ Lasers are being used in this experiment. They pick up movements in the earth.

▽ A tiltmeter measures changes in slope of the ground. If the ground tilts, the liquid runs from one container to the other.

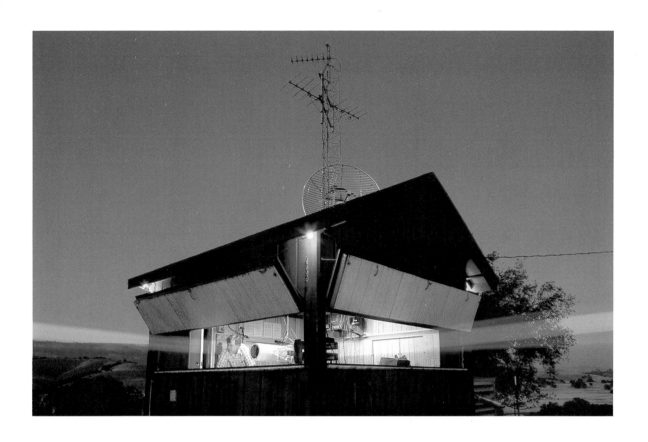

△ A beam of light from the laser is sent to a reflector and bounced back. From this scientists can measure movement in a fault.

Safety First

Many people who live in earthquake zones have houses which are built on solid rock. **Steel** rods may anchor the houses into the ground. When the ground shakes, the houses sway but do not collapse. Homes built on loose rock are more likely to fall down. During an earthquake people should keep away from buildings. If they are indoors, they should take shelter under a table.

▷ The Transamerica building in San Francisco is built to survive even the strongest earthquake.

▷ These buildings are built on an unsafe slope. They may fall down in an earthquake.

◁ To prevent earthquake damage some buildings are built on concrete pillars like these.

Great Earthquakes

- An earthquake struck Japan in 1923 when people were cooking their midday meals. Stoves fell over and many houses in the cities of Tokyo and Yokohama were burned to the ground.

- During the earthquake in 1906, in the city of San Francisco, the plates along the San Andreas fault moved more than 13 feet. This is about the length of a room.

- An earthquake off the coast of Alaska in 1964 was followed by tsunamis which were 220 feet high. That is higher than many church steeples. Tsunamis battered the coast and caused great destruction.

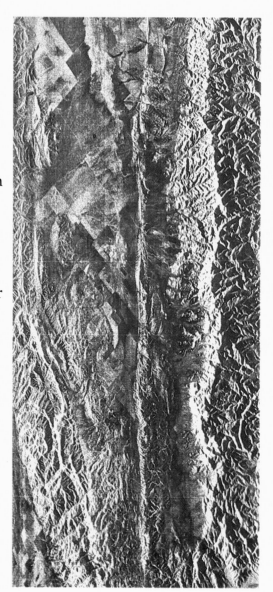

▷ This photograph was taken from a spacecraft. It shows the San Andreas Fault in North America.

Glossary

avalanche A large mass of snow or ice sliding down a mountainside.

coast The area of land that is next to the ocean.

collide To meet and hit together.

crust The outer hard surface which covers the Earth.

Earth The planet on which we live. The word "earth" is also the name for soil.

earthquake A sudden motion or trembling in the earth.

forecast To say what is going to happen.

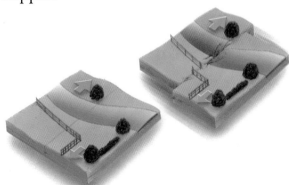

plates Pieces of the Earth's crust. They move very slowly on the hot rock beneath them.

rubble Broken stones or bricks.

seafloor The earth's surface covered by the sea or ocean.

seismograph A special instrument which records and measures earthquakes.

seismologist A person who studies earthquakes.

seismology The study of earthquakes.

steel A strong metal which is used in building.

valley A long usually narrow area of land lying between hills or mountains.

Index

Photographic credits: FLPA 21 (S. McCutcheon); GSF Picture Library 5, 11; Science Photo Library cover, 3, 16 (P. Menzel), 15, 27 (D. Parker) 23 (P. Ryan) 30 (Westinghouse Corporation); Zefa 8, 13, 19, 29.